the Midnight Mission

FROM DESPAIR TO RECOVERY

PHOTOGRAPHS BY LARRY BROWNSTEIN

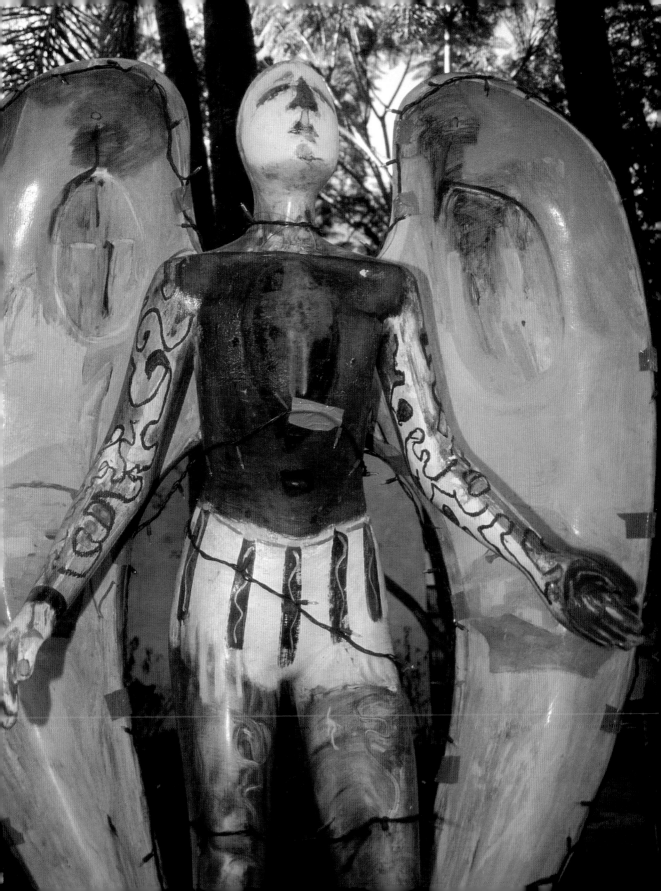

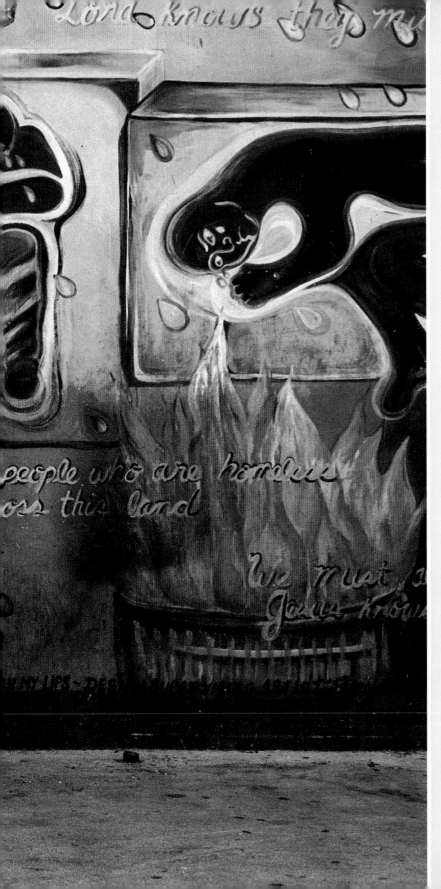

THE MIDNIGHT MISSION
From Despair to Recovery
Photographs by Larry Brownstein

THE MIDNIGHT MISSION
HOMELESS AWARENESS AND SPONSORSHIP CAMPAIGN
The Midnight Mission

AUTHOR : PHOTOGRAPHER : PHOTOGRAPHIC EDITOR
Larry Brownstein
www.larrybrownstein.com
larryb@larrybrownstein.com

CREATIVE EDITOR : DESIGN : ART DIRECTION
Mark Murphy
www.murphydesign.com

PUBLISHER
The Midnight Mission
www.midnightmission.com

To order, retail or wholesale, contact Ingrid Garcia
igarcia@midnightmission.com
888-624-9258 x 1243

FIRST EDITION PUBLISHED : 2005

Printed in China

ISBN 0-9742633-9-7

All human wisdom is summed up in two words,—wait and hope.

ALEXANDRE DUMAS THE ELDER

Statement of Purpose
To make available the necessities of life to homeless people: food, shelter, clothing, personal hygiene needs and medical care.

The Midnight Mission has been servicing the Los Angeles and Southern California homeless since 1914, when Tom Liddecoat opened the doors to The Midnight Mission as a refuge to the men of Skid Row. Many citizens have generously donated time, resources and financial support for our growing services. The following pages are an introduction to our family and a glimpse into some of the programs and events that take place on a minute by minute, hour by hour, day by day basis.

The Midnight Mission Statement of Purpose

TO OFFER A BRIDGE TO SELF-SUFFICIENCY
FOR HOMELESS PEOPLE THROUGH
COUNSELING, EDUCATION, TRAINING AND JOB PLACEMENT

TO MAKE AVAILABLE THE NECESSITIES OF LIFE TO HOMELESS PEOPLE:
FOOD, SHELTER, CLOTHING, PERSONAL HYGIENE NEEDS
AND MEDICAL CARE

TO OFFER THE 12-STEP APPROACH TO RECOVERY

TO SERVE HOMELESS PEOPLE WITH EMPATHY AND RESPECT,
WITHOUT SERMONIZING

TO PROVIDE FOR THE HOMELESS
AS AN INDEPENDENT SOCIAL SERVICE AGENCY

FIGURE 01

To ease another's heartache is to forget one's own.

ABRAHAM LINCOLN

LIFE'S MOST URGENT QUESTION IS: WHAT ARE YOU DOING FOR OTHERS?
// Dr. Martin Luther King, Jr. //

The Midnight Mission
converts
its parking lot into
one giant bedroom
in the evening.
It's called Safe Sleep
and many of the homeless
depend on it
to get
a safe night of sleep.
Security staff
supervises and ensures
people's safety
through the
night.

The Midnight Mission has over a hundred residents, some of whom have been there more than a year as they learn life skills, business skills, attend Twelve Steps meetings — Alcoholics Anonymous, Narcotics Anonymous, etc. — and work at The Mission.

There are jobs in food service, security, janitorial, front office, administrative, computer and even graphic design. Many of these jobs revolve around servicing the community of homeless people outside its doors. Breakfast, lunch and dinner are served to the homeless and the program participants. Haircuts, too, are offered to the homeless, as well as the residents. The Mission has a unique program called Safe Sleep — they convert their parking lot into a giant outdoor bedroom at night. Even the dining room is converted into a bedroom for homeless families. Just the basics are provided — a bed and blankets — but it provides a haven from the horror outside the doors.

The scale of the services provided is enormous.
As an example, according to the web site, the following services have been provided:

HAIRCUTS
66,343

MEALS SERVED
495,069

NIGHTS OF LODGING IN SAFE SLEEP
82,416

SHOWERS
63,392

IN MANY CASES RESIDENTS QUALIFY FOR DENTAL AND MEDICAL PROCEDURES, TOO.

FIGURE 02

Residents are counseled by personnel familiar with issues of chemical dependency and there is a palpable feeling of hope in the air as people recover from addictions, work as part of a community, learn new skills, repair old relationships and find new options in life. People advance through the program based upon their effort. Though not everybody sticks with the program, many do and learn new skills, get jobs and a new lease on life.

A few years ago my friend Clancy invited me to The Midnight Mission on a blustery Thanksgiving morning to help serve a holiday meal to the men, women and children of Skid Row. I wasn't really looking forward to the project, but I felt it was probably a good action to take. By the end of the day I was amazed to discover that The Mission was doing so much more than just feeding homeless people. I watched them actually changing lives and I've made it my favorite charity ever since. I've been involved with many activities through all the recent years and my admiration for The Mission's work continues to increase.

When I come to The Midnight Mission, I see people who once slept on cardboard boxes in dirty alleys now finding a way to live with a spark of dignity. I see discards of society gradually learning to live in a welfare-free, self-reliant, go-to-work world. I see fathers finally taking responsibility for their children and women freed from lethally abusive relationships. I see children with clean faces and clean clothes discovering something called "school." I see the most remarkable things, which make me proud to be a part of The Midnight Mission.

In the nearly 90 years of its existence, The Midnight Mission had undergone many changes to keep up with the changing face of home-lessness and despair. Building a Home for Hope is the latest and best of these changes. With our help, The Mission will be able to reach out to more people who desperately need emergency assistance. More importantly, it will continue the life-saving programs that have changed so many lives.

NOT HE WHO HAS MUCH IS RICH, BUT HE WHO GIVES MUCH.
// Erich Fromm //

It was dark and eerie on
Skid Row.
The dawn was breaking
and I was weary
as I approached
this man.
I asked,
"How are you?"
and he answered,
"I am blessed."
He had his Bible handy
and told me that Jesus had
sent me to give him
a few dollars.

Alcohol and narcotics addictions have, for many years, been a growing problem both in size and scope. The reason for the addictions remains a puzzle to most of the community and why people should continue to use substances that are destroying them is an enigma to nearly everyone.

First, there should be an understanding that there is a difference between addictions. It is relatively safe to say that any significant use of a barbiturate will bring about a physical addiction in the user. Alcohol, however, will bring about an addictive reaction in only about ten percent of drinkers. And, the alcohol addiction is further divided. The more common is the psychological addiction, which requires alcohol to satisfy deep emotional conflict. Over a period of time this can eventually evolve into a physical addiction, a more lethal condition.

The original treatment centers were created to withdraw addicts from physical addiction to alcohol. As one authority described it, "…put ten drug addicts into a room for ten days and you will have ten very sick addicts. Put ten physically addicted alcoholics into a room for ten days and you will have four or five dead."

The classic horror stories of alcoholism…convulsions, delirium tremens and the rest…are symptoms of withdrawal from the physical addiction. In the early days of AA, members would carry a pint of whiskey when calling on a new man in the event he began to go into the DTs.

It is safe to say that no one ever starts out with the intention of becoming an addict. Nearly always the substance — whether drugs or alcohol — begins as a feel-good experience with few significant drawbacks. But if the user gets the euphoria that may be part of its use, the pleasure eventually turns into dependence and addiction. "Quitting" becomes more and more difficult and time after time the user's mind rationalizes… "I'll just use it again this one time to get over feeling bad and then I'll stop."

Little by little he or she goes down the slippery slope and one day it's too late. It is almost impossible to break the addiction because "sobriety" becomes unbearable. What used to be the euphoria of the substance now has become the only agent to remove deep emotional desperation.

There have been writings to describe addictions for thousands of years and endless attempts have been made to overcome them. There has never been any appreciable result except for two brief periods in history. One came in the 1840's when a small group of alcoholics, calling themselves the Washingtonians, brought about the sobriety of literally tens of thousands of alcohol addicts, through the sharing of "one alcoholic to another." After several years of great success, they decided to widely expand their efforts and to help all sorts of people with all sorts of problems. Within three years they were extinct, and certainly most of them died drunken deaths.

The other example, of course, is Alcoholics Anonymous. Beginning with a small segment of the Oxford Movement in 1935, it eventually has grown into an entity of its own, containing perhaps two million sober alcoholics in 134 countries around the earth. Its therapy deals with the problem that has always doomed the recovery of alcoholics and addicts. That problem is the inherent belief in every addict that "my case is different"…and it is based on the knowledge that "drinking (or drugs) is not really the problem… merely takes away the only thing that makes me feel good and returns me to pain and anxiety. They just don't understand!"

The methodology of AA is quite simple. It is based on identification, as opposed to instruction or advice from well-meaning but obviously non-understanding sources. This identification is in being able to convey the same secret feelings and emotions that the user thought were unique unto him or her.

The program of AA is not unique as such, but is extremely effective for people who have seemed to be hopeless. This is the result when "advice" — which every alcoholic or addict has had enough of to last a thousand years - becomes "meaningful information" which can be accepted. The AA members are directed and encouraged to take a series of actions that eventually brings about a significant change in perception. If the mark of the alcoholic or the addict is that he must take the substance that makes an unbearable reality quickly change to a pleasurable condition, the mark of a successful AA is that he continues to take the actions that slowly change an unbearable reality into an pleasurable condition. With identification, such things almost routinely take place.

Because of this, alcoholics who also had severe gambling problems asked AA to allow the formation of a new organization to be known as Gamblers Anonymous that would use the 12 steps promulgated by AA changing "alcohol" to "gambling." Later alcoholics who were also narcotics addicts brought the same request, resulting in Narcotics Anonymous. Soon thereafter came Cocaine Anonymous, Overeaters Anonymous and many more. Although the 12 steps provide a therapy for recovery, all these programs are successful because they allow members to identify with others who have had the same problem and who can demonstrate a solution.

The great problem for many alcoholics who "sample" AA is that the 12 steps do not apparently deal with the problems at hand. As a result, many do not stay or even make any significant effort to put the suggestions to use. A truism of AA is that the more desperate newcomers are, the better chance for recovery because they will be more flexible in dealing with their disbelief and may take actions even if they think it won't work. The magic here is that one doesn't have to believe in AA — you just have to do it. Eventually the relief comes and it seems like a miracle.

An example of the positive/negative aspects of alcohol in an alcoholic is a brief look at my own life. Raised in a very good Norwegian Lutheran home in Wisconsin, I was nevertheless always somewhat restless and eager to push the envelope. When the war started in 1941, I was fascinated…and by the end of 1942 — at the age of 15 — I told my mother I was going

to visit my aunt in Superior, Wisconsin. She packed my little bag and gave me bus fare, which I then used to hitchhike to San Francisco. I was very naïve and inexperienced, but fortunately got a ride from Minneapolis all the way to San Francisco with a Navy man returning to his ship.

He counseled me that I probably could not be accepted into the Marines (as was my plan), but by stating that I was 16 I might be able to get a seaman's papers in the Merchant Marines. I followed his advice at the Coast Guard office on Market Street and was issued the documents that would enable me to ship out. (They were very short of men because so many had gone into the Navy …they would take almost anyone who could walk.)

My first trip, on a Liberty Ship to the Pacific, was a most eye-opening experience. I was thrown in with the dregs of the seven seas, it seemed, and I was treated like a dumb kid — which I was, of course. But in the course of the first voyage, I was introduced to my first drink of alcohol. It made me throw up, to the laughter of the old salts. I kept trying to drink, over a period of days, so that the guys would think I was a "man." As we entered Pearl Harbor, I held my first drink down and for the first time experienced the euphoric relief that alcohol provides that ten percent of drinkers who respond to it.

Later in the war, when I was 17, I went into the Navy. At the end of the war, some special GI tests allowed me to enter the University of Wisconsin - despite still only being a Junior in high school. I won some trophies for the University and went out into the world as a newspaper sports writer and eventually into advertising and public relations for several corporations.

All these years I enjoyed the feelings of completeness that alcohol gave me. I think it is safe to say that alcohol was the best friend I ever had.

Eventually, however, I began to lose control over how often and how much I would drink. But, at the same time, living without alcohol was unbearable. I changed a few jobs over this and moved from city to city. My wife and children joined me without complaint, although we would temporarily live a hand-to-mouth existence until I got another good job.

Finally, I went down for the last time. Working on the Borden Cow ads in Dallas, my drinking now caused me to miss work until I was discharged. My wife got some advice from a new organization (at that time) called Alanon, which indicated she should take the children and leave. My car was taken back by the company and in a matter of a few days I had no place to turn. A friend gave me a car to deliver to Los Angeles and paid me a few dollars. I got drunk in El Paso, but somehow muddled out of there. The next night I was drunk in Phoenix but this time lost the car with all my personal effects, papers, clothing and identification. That night I got into a loud argument with a police officer and was put in jail overnight. About midnight, apparently, I was sick, and inadvertently threw up on another inmate's bunk. This so enraged him, he knocked me down and kicked at me several times…taking out my front teeth.

The next morning I was released on the streets of Phoenix sick, bloody, broke, with torn clothes and in total despair. I hustled $20 from a kindly person there and took the bus to Los Angeles. Within a matter of a few days I had received some money from the program director of KFWB (a man to whom I had given his first job in Texas), drank heavily, got into trouble at an all-night theater…and at 6:30 a.m. on a cold rainy morning was thrown out of The Midnight Mission by two men whom I had engaged in a fight.

Thirty-one years old, weighing about 125 pounds, no front teeth, in dirty, torn clothing with blood stains on the shirt…there was absolutely no hope or future. Complete desperation. I could think of no one — including my parents - who would accept a collect phone call. There was no way out.

I thought perhaps the only chance would be to get some money from that ridiculous thing called Alcoholics Anonymous, which I had previously sampled and had instantly realized had nothing to offer a person of my intellect and state of emotional upheaval. In talking to another derelict outside The Mission that morning, I found the closest AA was at Wilshire and Fairfax. I've often been grateful I did not know how far it would be, because I started walking there, a trip, which seemed to never end. It turned out to be 72 long blocks (which I ascertained in an auto some years later), but there was no place to stop, so I just kept trudging until I got there.

I had no intention of finding anything there except perhaps some financial aid, but in the coming days and weeks and months I was led, directed and impelled to do things I had never done before, i.e., the actions of AA. I found a sponsor who, although seemingly tough, helped me to identify the real nature of the problem for the first time, and, thereby, was able to get me to do things that I did not as yet believe in.

That was 47 years ago and the interim years have been quite varied. I started as a dishwasher in a Sunset Boulevard restaurant, worked through stops as a janitor, a busboy and finally got a job as a "beginning" writer. Using the emotional tools I learned through my sponsor, I eventually became ad director at a medical corporation, helped found "Boss Radio," the most successful station of its kind in the 1960's, became a PR account executive at Bowes Advertising and eventually wound up as Marketing Director for a Beverly Hills publishing firm.

Through a very strange series of events, in February 1974, I became the Managing Director of The Midnight Mission. It has been my great experience to continue at this facility, making use of the teachings I have found in AA to try to help men and women who still suffer and die from this strange malady called alcoholism.

Though I have lived in L.A. for over 20 years I had little idea of the extent of homelessness in the city. As this project progressed I came face to face with numerous stories of human misery. Fortunately, I heard and saw even more inspirational stories about people turning their lives around, leaving drugs behind them and rebuilding family relationships. I don't consider myself an expert on homelessness. My goal in this book is to share my experiences with the hope that increased awareness may help the homeless.

Many people try to avoid looking at the homeless and unfortunate people walking around their city. I, too, avoided looking. Yet I now know that this population of the unfortunate is quite diverse in ethnic backgrounds, age, gender and family status. I had a preconception that most homeless people were mentally ill. Many are mentally ill, yet I also met many eloquent and intelligent people who ran into bad luck and had no support system. One man comes to mind, a 30-year old man who had recently lost his job with a video production company. He was an expert in the use of Final Cut Pro — software for video editing —and found himself on the streets after his company was bought out and he lost his job. He was articulate and intelligent and was looking for work, despite the challenges imposed by being on the street. Another man comes to mind - a purchasing manager who worked for companies such as Honeywell and Sylvania whose luck changed as the result of a serious car accident and a divorce. He, too, is clearly a capable and well-spoken person and he is looking for work despite the difficulty of living out of a beat-up car that doubles as his office.

Another myth I entered into this project with is that all homeless people are depressed and beaten down. It is certainly true that there is much of this and many people die on the streets for lack of food, healthcare, etc. At the same time I learned that many people on the streets, though deprived of housing and many things considered basic necessities, are mentally healthy. Some of them have many friends, often other homeless people. Quite often my greeting of "How are you?" would be answered with, "I am blessed."

Though homelessness is a central theme of the book it should be mentioned that some of the people depicted in this book may not be homeless. For exam-

---

Information about the homeless according to the Weingart Center's website:

A } FAMILIES REPRESENT A GROWING PERCENTAGE OF THE HOMELESS POPULATION WITH ESTIMATES RANGING FROM 20% TO 43%.

B } ABOUT ONE-HALF OF HOMELESS ADULTS ARE HIGH SCHOOL GRADUATES.

C } 80,000 PEOPLE ARE HOMELESS EACH NIGHT IN LOS ANGELES COUNTY.

D } ABOUT ONE-QUARTER OF HOMELESS ADULTS ARE PHYSICALLY DISABLED.

E } VETERANS ARE ABOUT TWICE AS LIKELY TO BE HOMELESS.

FIGURE 03

ple, groups of people are depicted waiting for a Thanksgiving meal or entry to Santa's Village, etc. It is likely that many of these people are in low-income housing. Yet they are served by The Midnight Mission or other shelters and therefore are depicted in this book. Others are depicted pushing shopping carts and it is likely, but not certain, that such a person is homeless.

One definition of a homeless person is: an individual who lacks a fixed, regular and adequate nighttime residence. In the Skid Row area many people who are not officially homeless have a roof over their heads (though many would debate whether it is an "adequate" residence) but need to use most of their financial resources to afford this residence and thus may soon be homeless themselves.

It would be easy to focus on the depressing aspect of some of these images - people drinking in alleyways, smoking crack etc. But I would like to think that most readers will realize that the heart of this book is about the people who have experienced the hell of the streets and are now serving the community themselves. People such as Barry Liss, a one-time resident at The Midnight Mission, who is now a successful recording artist and plays for the community at holiday events. Jeff Mandel and Don Halfenberg, both of whom have been homeless, now work at The Mission as counselors. Clancy Imislund, once homeless, has served as Managing Director of The Midnight Mission for over 30 years.

Most homeless people are camera shy. Undoubtedly, some are too embarrassed by their situation. A few people have told me that they wouldn't want family members seeing published pictures of them. Many of them expressed their fears of being found by the police, loan sharks, etc., if their picture were published. It is for this reason that names are changed or omitted.

I often joined outreach workers from various organizations as an opportunity to meet homeless people. For readability, their names are often left out of the text, though this book benefited greatly from their assistance.

OCTOBER 19TH

Today was my first day working on The Midnight Mission project.
It was eye opening.

I met Sammy, one of the kitchen staff who prepare 1,500 meals a day. He told me about how after many years of living on the streets he found God. Now, in his spare time, he preaches out on the streets.

I met Norman, who greeted me with the confidence of a corporate CEO, with an alpha-male demeanor and a handshake to match. He told me he had had numerous academic and athletic scholarships and an advanced degree in Biochemistry. After graduation, he was derailed by cocaine use. He was eloquent about how God brought him to the streets and now to The Midnight Mission to be an example to people and to show them that there is a way out of drug use.

Later in the morning I attended a graduation ceremony for nine residents of The Midnight Mission who had completed the Business Skills program. I photographed the ceremony that was attended by the whole community — more than 100 residents and staff showing their support and enthusiasm for each graduate.

After the ceremony everyone was in good spirits and enjoyed cake in the dining room. I was told: "This is a dangerous time. They think they have achieved something and they think they've put their problems behind them. That's when people lose their guard and relapse."

In the afternoon, I was escorted around "Skid Row" by Larry, whose nickname is The Shark, as he was once a pool hall hustler. Larry's story unfolded over the course of several hours as we walked around some of the nightmarish streets around The Mission.

Larry's uncle ran a bar and a pool hall. Larry developed excellent skills at a young age and his uncle began to make money betting on him. At 17, Larry hit the road to hustle people in pool halls. Larry got so good that he ended up playing in televised world championship tournaments. Everything was going his way — he had "money and girls." At some point he found himself drinking in bars regularly, he crossed an invisible line and things began to fall apart. Today, he works in Public Relations at The Midnight Mission and believes it has saved his life.

Larry and I walked around the surreal streets of Skid Row and he pointed out things that my untrained eye would not have seen — outhouses that are used more as bordellos and shoot-up rooms, congregations of people shooting up heroine or crack, and the distinguished-looking man with dreadlocks, wearing a long wool coat and a fancy hat, dealing drugs. We avoided several streets, as Larry advised that they were too dangerous.

OCTOBER 20TH

*But today I am mentally scattered and physically weak, just as I would imagine
many of the homeless feel.*

I am wiped out. Yesterday, I did such a good job of not appearing anxious that I even fooled myself. I'm a street-wise Brooklyn boy, I told myself, so I could certainly handle Los Angeles. But I have to admit that I wouldn't feel so exhausted if I hadn't been scared.

I shook hands with many homeless and schizophrenic people yesterday. It seemed like the polite thing to do. I figured that most of these people could often go a week without experiencing a touch of human kindness, so I thought a handshake was a small gesture I could provide.

But, perhaps, that was a mistake. Is it possible that by shaking their hands I took on some of their *energy*? I don't usually talk about people's *energy* in that way but I don't have a better explanation.

OCTOBER 26TH

*In America, getting on in the world means
getting out of the world we have known before. // Ellery Sedgwick //*

The streets were less crowded than usual, perhaps because of a sweep by the cops. It could also be related to the storm that was threatening. Perhaps many of the homeless found their way to shelters for the night to keep dry.

A Mexican man told us proudly that he had been a gang member and had served time in San Quentin. We got to know him a bit and he became comfortable enough with us to share a secret. He reached inside his mouth and pulled out a pea-sized, red object. It was heroin wrapped inside a balloon. He was selling it. He kept it in his mouth in case the police came by. He let me photograph it, though, he said, that was enough evidence to send him back to prison.

I walked by a seedy little hotel that doubles as a crack den. Surprisingly, it is located across the street from the police station. On another corner was the Union Rescue Mission. A little further down was San Julian Park, crowded inside and out with more than a hundred homeless men and women. Among the lost souls filling in time in the park was an angel. It was a statue, over six feet tall with a wingspan nearly as wide. This was one of the angels commissioned by the Community of Angels public works project several years ago. I wondered, did any of the souls sitting in the park receive any comfort from the statue? Were their own guardian angels at their side whispering words of comfort to them?

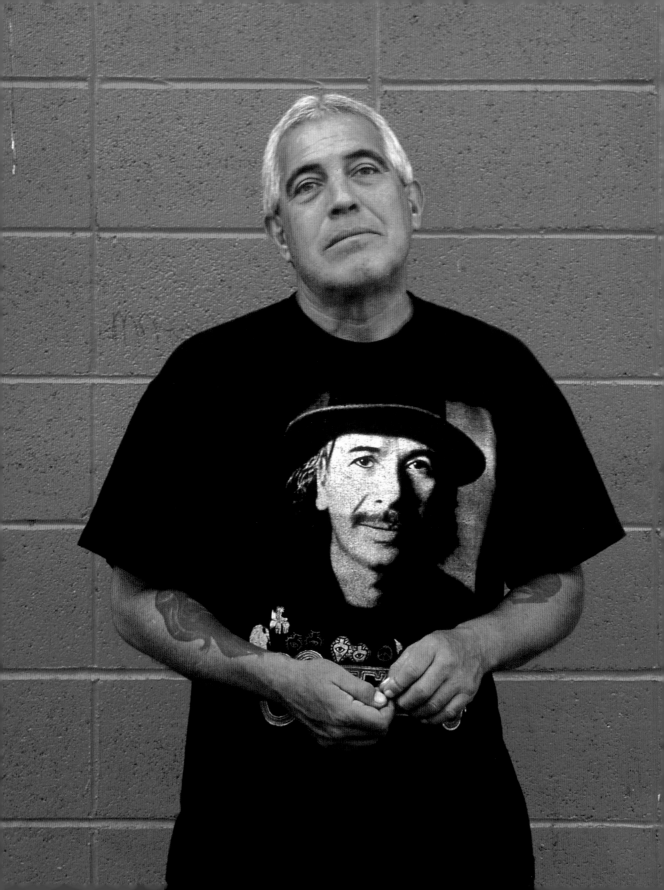

NOVEMBER 3RD

A block away a woman chatted me up for just a minute but she summed things up
very simply: "This is hell. Welcome to hell. Either you fight back or you lay down and die."

The streets were quiet again today. Early in the month many people have money from a variety of sources — welfare, disability, etc. For some it doesn't last long, perhaps only a few days. For others, it is a chance to sleep in a hotel for a few days or perhaps a chance to buy drugs.

I spotted a woman wearing a red and black dress, a shiny, gold jacket and a straw hat. I was interested in her but it was difficult to make contact with her. Her attention was somewhere else and she hardly noticed my presence even though I spoke directly to her. She dug into her purse and found a glass tube and then stuffed something in one end. She lit up and started smoking the pipe and quickly her intensity melted away. She began to sway and turn like a fashion model. In just a minute or two, she had been transported to another world.

NOVEMBER 5TH

I accompanied outreach workers from the Los Angeles Homeless Services Agency today on their rounds.
They visit, chat, give out water and offer referrals for services — hot meals, places to sleep, etc.

We went to the Los Angeles River near the Cesar Chavez Bridge. It's more of a cement canal than a river and it conjured up in my mind scenes from several movies shot there, including a chase scene in a Schwarzenegger movie.

In this area there were overpasses under which several homeless people made their homes. It was the Beverly Hills of homelessness. Leroy has made his home here for more than 20 years. Peering inside a locked gate we could see that he had a lot of room and a lot of furniture. He unlocked the gate and let himself out to speak with us. He was glad to speak with the outreach workers with whom he chatted like old friends.

Under the same overpass but across the train tracks we spoke with Nacho, who also locked himself and his pit bull inside a gate. Walking between the train tracks and the river we ran into a woman who was new to the area. They discussed getting her into an SRO (single room occupancy, a subsidized room, hotel), her medications and transportation to an upcoming doctor's appointment. She pointed out where she slept and we went to see: a little structure built around a storm drain that cuts a horizontal notch in the 45-degree wall that surrounds the river. Some lumber and office cubicle partitions gave her some added shelter. She was reading a book with the provocative title *Universal Lexical Encyclopedia*. We asked her about it and she said it was an electronics book. She told us as we left, "The left side of my brain is damaged. Entropy is setting in."

Next, we went to visit a large homeless encampment miles away in the Wilmington area. Bordered by an oil field on one side and the Los Angeles River on the other side with the freeway passing overhead we found a little oasis of trees. As we entered the forest, the bright colors of plastic tarps became visible. One man was sleeping and another man, Dennis, was organizing his things. Dennis took us on a tour of his place and pointed out such treasures as brass candelabra, huge marble chess pieces and backgammon sets. He had piles of electronic circuit boards. He gave us a gift - an old plaque of Colonel Sanders (the face behind Kentucky Fried Chicken) walking hand in hand with a boy and a girl.

He expounded upon a variety of topics, always with an interesting point of view. He took us to a beat-up statue of Jesus on the cross and explained to us that God would not want us to remember his son dying on the crucifix; he'd want us to remember his son's message of peace and love. Dennis was both brilliant and charismatic. We all wondered how he became homeless.

NOVEMBER 28TH

It was a beautiful, sunny morning with just a little chill in the air. At 8:00 a.m. people are already lining up on Los Angeles Street for their Thanksgiving feast. There is electricity in the air.

I was told that Thanksgiving plans begin months in advance and that program participants were up at 3:00 a.m. preparing for the festivities. The scale of the effort is enormous. Just the artwork lining both sides of 4th Street represents a huge effort! In the dining room I saw a dozen volunteers just cutting the pumpkin and pecan pies! There are more than a hundred volunteers assisting the staff.

Near the serving area I heard a woman singing, "Use me. Oh Lord. I stand by you. And here I'll abide." The song was familiar to me as an occasional visitor at the Agape Center of Religious Science, as it is sung during services. I spoke with her about Agape and its pastor, whom we both admire and I took a picture of her. Later I was told that she was Elaine Hendrix, who has a leading role in the television show Joan of Arcadia.

Other celebrities were there including Lou Gossett Jr. and Antonio Villaraigosa. Dick Van Dyke, who has long been an avid supporter of The Midnight Mission was there, too, giving out candy.

Thousands of delicious meals of turkey, ham, bread, mashed potatoes, gravy and stuffing were served, an excellent band rocked out, thousands of pairs of shoes were given away as well as clothes piled high on several dozen tables. Kids played on a moonbounce and had their faces painted. Free phone calls were provided on a half-dozen cell phones and bags of canned food were given out as people left.

Everyone was in great spirits. If only every day could be Thanksgiving!

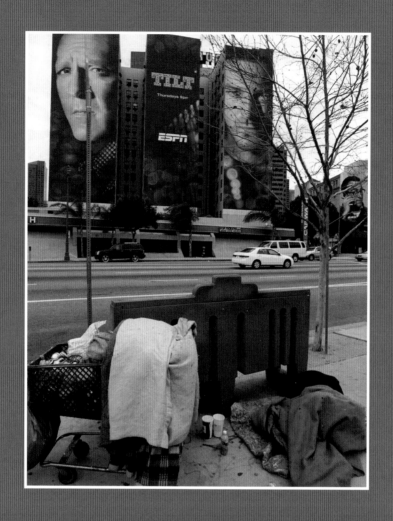

NOVEMBER 29TH

...forced to work, forced to do your best, will breed in you temperance and self-control, diligence and strength of will, cheerfulness and content... // Charles Kingsley //

I was taking pictures right outside The Mission today. A man who was clearly not homeless asked me what I was doing. I get asked this quite often — some people are just curious, some are merely suspicious but others are hostile.

This guy had a friendly smile so I answered and asked him what he was doing. He told me he was a reporter for Dateline NBC and that for four months his team was busy documenting the homeless problem. I asked him where the video cameras were and he replied that all the cameras were hidden.

I wasn't sure whether to believe him. I have spoken to many people who are out of touch with reality. So I asked him to show me some press credentials and he declined. Was he for real or not? I'll have to tune in to Dateline NBC to find out.

DECEMBER 1ST

Once again, I joined the outreach workers from the Los Angeles Homeless Services Agency on a visit to the Wilmington encampment.

Arriving there we saw signs posted all over warning that the area would be cleared out in several days. We visited with several of the residents, one of whom was busy stripping metal off of heavy equipment that he would sell to a recycling center.

As we were leaving we saw Sharon, who said she needed help. She grabbed a knife and started cutting open her right pant leg revealing a terribly swollen and discolored leg. She explained that she had been riding her bicycle and was hit by a car that left the scene. She thought she was fine but then several days later began having trouble with her leg. She has been to the local hospital but is not happy with having to wait and doesn't want to let them cut her leg open to explore, as they suggested. No X-rays have been taken. She doesn't have identification and that makes it harder to get services.

She spoke quickly and forcefully telling us her whole story — she used to make good money as a dockworker. She worked 12-hour shifts and sometimes used speed to make it through a long day. Now she is 27 years old and homeless. I gave her a few dollars thinking it would help her to get bus fare to the hospital. She assured me that she would use it just for that. Or would she use the money for speed?

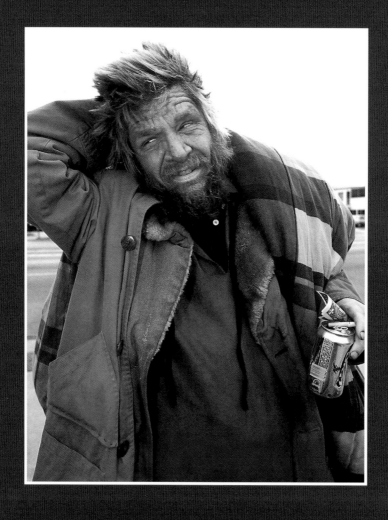

DECEMBER 4TH

It appears that I am now noticing homeless people in places where they were once invisible to me.

Yesterday I drove to my local gym and a homeless woman was there with five shopping carts loaded with stuffed plastic bags. They had holes in them and she told me it was from the rats where she slept.

Today my wife and I took a friend to Venice Beach, where we went to an art gallery to see an exhibit of blown-glass sculptures by Chihuly. Impressive work with impressive price tags to match - one installation was marked at $337,000. On the way home, we saw a homeless man whom I spoke with. His name was Evan and he was focused on getting a match to light his cigarette but he allowed me to take a few pictures. He seemed to enjoy modeling and he struck some interesting poses.

DECEMBER 8TH

Someone rode towards me on a bicycle. I asked to take a photo. "No thanks. The CIA already has one on file," he told me.

I returned to the Wilmington encampment today. A guy I hadn't seen before must have seen me parking my car nearby as he greeted me aggressively, "Ah, Mr. BMW. Nice camera. I could get 50 bucks for that." But before long he was telling me about his recurring dream: He steps into a house with a two-foot thick layer of dust, etc. I quickly suspected it was fiction he was making up as he went along. It took a few attempts to extract myself from his storytelling; he must have really needed to speak to someone.

I suddenly found myself confronted by a pit bull, its eyes flaring with hate, straining at its leash to get a piece of me. The owner could barely hold him back. Once the danger was over, I immediately searched around for a weapon, in case the situation arose again. With all the junk around I thought it would be easy but it wasn't. I settled for a hefty branch.

{Later, it was explained to me that the pit bull was a good indicator that a drug dealer was nearby. The dealer can be in possession of a great deal of drugs and cash and the dog provides some protection.}

I gave out photos to the people I met and photographed the first time I was here. This created some good will and the next thing I knew I was sitting in a "tent" talking. I was at home with the homeless. We talked politics and listened to harmonica music. I was told that a sometimes resident, Steve Kemp, died here a few nights ago and it was related to drug use. I asked what drug was involved and was told, "It's not the drugs, it's stopping the drugs that kills you. It's like the people leaping out of the windows of the World Trade Center — it's not the fall, it's the stop at the end of the fall that kills you."

DECEMBER 15TH

*Hungry not only for bread — but hungry for love. Naked not only for clothing —
but naked for human dignity and respect. Homeless not only for want of a room of bricks —
but homeless because of rejection. // Mother Teresa //*

The Midnight Mission Thrift Store, in Huntington Park, operates differently from other thrift stores. Much of the merchandise — household goods, clothing, furniture, etc. — is provided to those who come in with vouchers from any of several counseling programs, with the goal of helping people transition into housing.

There is also a large showroom that works much as a conventional thrift shop. The store is strategically located in Huntington Park, because of the community's low median income, yet I spoke with a woman who came all the way from Long Beach because she likes shopping here.

DECEMBER 16TH

When you do nothing, you feel overwhelmed and powerless. But when you get involved, you feel the sense of hope and accomplishment that comes from knowing you are working to make things better. // Pauline R. Kezer //

'Tis not the season to be jolly on the mean streets of Skid Row. The buzz at The Mission this morning was about four stabbings during the night. I am not surprised. I have come to learn that, with some people, there is a seething anger that can erupt quickly.

This morning I went out with William, an outreach worker who is also a resident at The Midnight Mission. I took a few photos of a man sleeping. While I looked through the camera some guy came up to me with a story about my taking a picture of him a few days earlier, which I'm pretty sure was a lie. He spoke so loudly that the sleeping man awoke and launched into an instant rage about my taking his picture without permission. He was yelling for the film, "If I don't get that film one of us is going to the hospital and it ain't gonna be me." It's a good thing William, a big guy, was with me. Finally, a $5 bill got us out of there safely. My heart was racing.

DECEMBER 19TH

It's the last Sunday before Christmas and a busy day on Skid Row. Another homeless shelter had its big event for mothers with children, complete with Christmas carols, prayers, Santa Claus and celebrities. Perhaps a hundred volunteers gave out toys to the kids.

Hours later, The Midnight Mission hosted a Vietnamese Church group that brought food and presents for the homeless and sang Christmas songs, too. They gave out blankets and sleeping bags and served hot soup. A veteran of the situation informed me that some of the sleeping bags would be traded for a quick high, but many will benefit from a warm night's sleep!

A block away from The Midnight Mission a van pulled up and gave away dozens of meals in Styrofoam containers.

I heard much Skid Row lore about The Ten-Dollar Man, Father Chase, etc. Every year around this time The Ten-Dollar Man comes and gives out thousands of dollars, in $10 bills, outdoing Father Chase who is around most Sundays giving out $1 bills but occasionally giving a hundred dollar bill when the spirit moves him.

I heard a story about an old couple that came last year around Christmas with chicken dinners. They were mobbed by the crowds and ended up in the hospital.

DECEMBER 21ST

Before long the sun will go down and the magnificent Christmas light display will go on.
I am grateful to be able to look forward to such a simple pleasure.

There was a buzz about The Ten Dollar Man coming to The Midnight Mission today. I asked the Midnight Mission security staff some questions about it and found them surprisingly tight-lipped. It was clear that they were coached not to tell too much. They didn't want people with guns showing up to mug The Ten Dollar Man. Long lines had already formed when I first checked in at The Mission at 8:00 a.m., but no one would say exactly when The Ten Dollar Man was expected.

So I went exploring the streets and was invited to photograph Loretta in her tent but only after she had a chance to clean it up a little bit. Amongst her possessions were a Barbie doll and some children's books she is using to teach herself to read.

Later I met Annie who also had a tent. She had a nice place for herself and her man with blankets, foam pads, reading material and bottles of water.

By the time I returned to The Mission in the afternoon, The Ten Dollar Man had come and gone having given away thousands of dollars. The security staff looked exhausted. It must have been quite a task trying to keep order.

The traffic — cars and pedestrians — in downtown is truly awful this time of year. Once I learned I had missed The Ten Dollar Man I immediately knew I needed some quiet, space, solitude and beauty. I am writing this from the immaculate lawns of the Mormon Temple in Westwood. I can feel myself decompressing. But, sadly, so many of the folks I see on Skid Row never have that chance to decompress. Sitting in the TV Room at The Midnight Mission is the closest thing to relaxation for many of them.

On December 22, National Public Radio carried the story of The Ten Dollar Man. They called him the El Dorado Elf and said he had given away $15,000.

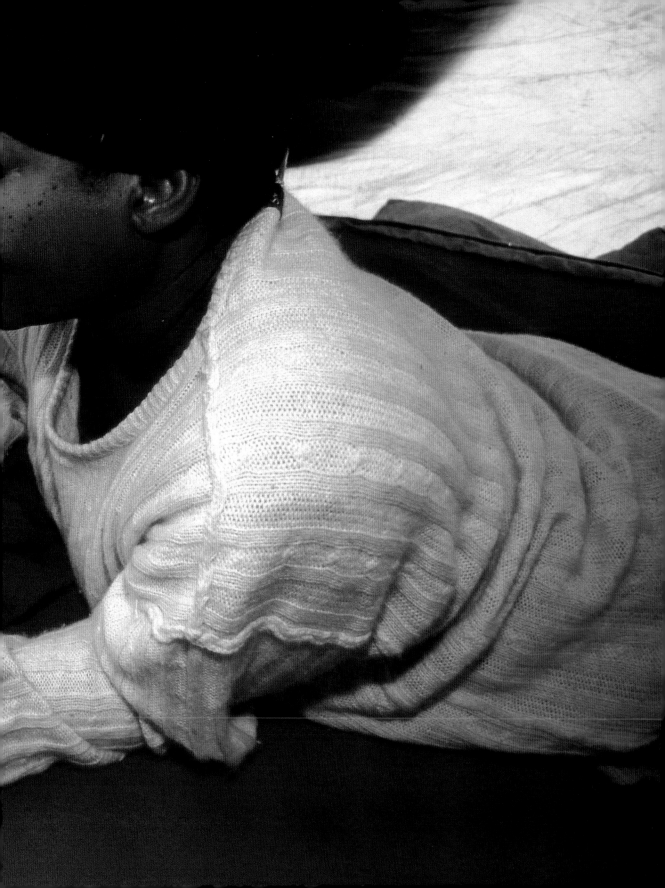

DECEMBER 25TH

Here, Christmas was celebrated as I think Jesus would have wanted it to be: by serving meals to thousands of hungry souls and giving toys to thousands of children.

~

As the crowds lined up for Christmas breakfast at The Midnight Mission, I had a philosophical discussion with Tyrone — a program resident who has become The Mission's computer guru and graphic artist. We talked about self-will versus God's will and how difficult it is to discern the difference. We agreed that if it were easy to tell the difference "there would be no game."

The Mission's parking lot was converted into Santa's Village and 4th Street was converted into a giant dining hall. On one side of 4th Street kids lined up with their parents to enter Santa's Village where they were greeted by Santa and Mrs. Claus and allowed to select three presents. On the other side of 4th Street people lined up for their meal. Everyone was welcome to a meal and many of the low-income neighbors came and enjoyed the meal along with the homeless.

After photographing for a while I needed to eat. I enjoyed a great meal: eggs, sausage, potatoes, biscuit and gravy. I spoke with a man originally from Sri Lanka who said he comes to the Mission every Christmas as he has done since he was "born again." A fellow sat down and I asked, "How are you?" He answered, "I am blessed."

Another man sat down and when we shook hands I felt like a small child again as my hand was lost in his huge one. It reminded me that not everyone makes their living from "brain work" and that I am indeed a 'stranger in a strange land' when in this environment. Yet, as we spoke, I found him bringing the conversation to cosmology — the age and size of the universe and our relative insignificance in terms of size and lifespan.

That evening my wife and I attended a 50th anniversary party at a Yacht Club in Newport Beach. It was a black tie affair with a lavish meal, floral arrangements so large that they had to be suspended above the tables so people could see one another and even chocolate bars with pictures of the happy couple on the wrapper. It was a jarring contrast from the morning!

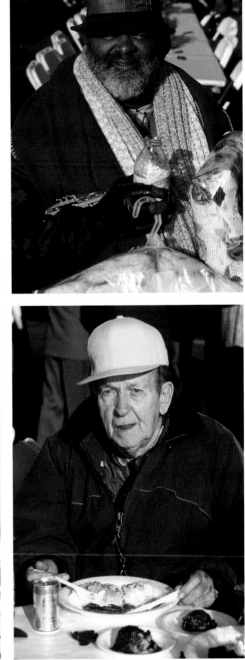

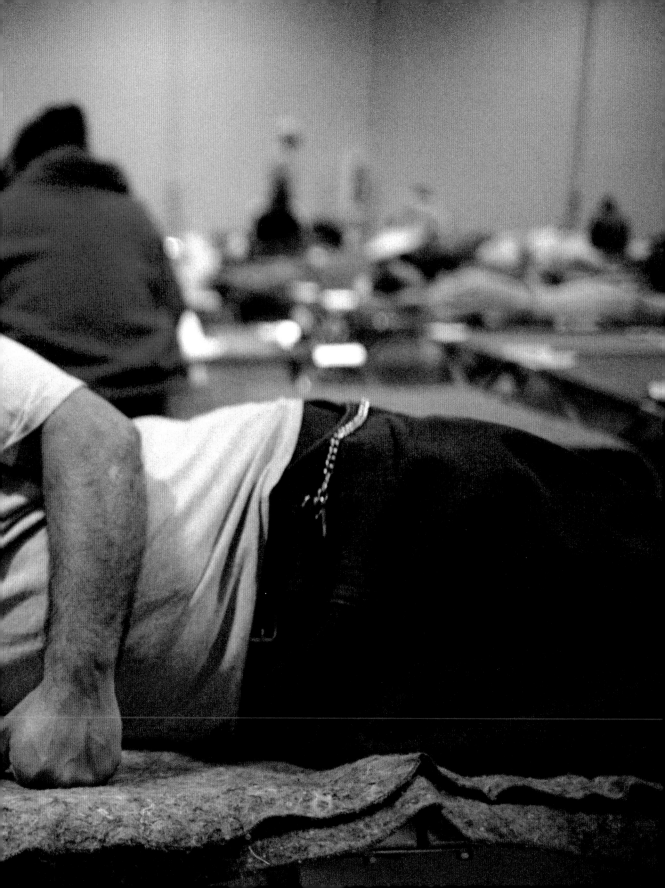

∾

Santa Monica, dubbed by one radio host as "the home of the homeless" is quite tolerant of a homeless population though far less so than in the recent past. For example, organizations such as Food Not Bombs and Shelter come only sporadically to feed the homeless as they fear being cited, though in years past such organizations openly served food to the homeless.

Pacific Park is perched on a bluff with a glorious view of Pacific Coast Highway, the beach and the ocean looking to the west. To the east there are expensive hotels, fine restaurants and architecturally distinctive office buildings. The park itself is one of the jewels of Los Angeles with a promenade lined by imposing palm trees on each side providing stunning views even when not looking out over the ocean. It is a popular spot with locals, Japanese tourists and the homeless.

"The Mission saved my life. I was roaming around downtown. I spent eight years downtown. I was homeless, meaning I had no permanent residence. I used to hustle and do things on the street to try to get money. I would do scams and get some money and stay in one of the flop hotels downtown. I was selling dope and smoking dope and everything was revolving around drugs - cocaine in particular. Finally, things just got out of hand. I had people looking to shoot me. I had the police on my tail. Everything just snowballed out of control."

"I went to The Mission under false pretenses. I went in to just hide for a while, to get healthy, get some food in me. I knew I would get a bed, a shower and some clothes. But I told them if I go back out on the street again I wouldn't live very much longer and that part was very much true. I would have gotten shot or thrown in jail."

"I found that I liked it. Once I got away from being loaded every day, things started to get a little clearer. I started out cleaning toilets just like everyone else but I knew I wanted to make it up the ranks. I was a security guard for a little while but I made it up to the front desk."

While working the front desk he became friendly with Larry Adamson, who at the time was a board member. Barry was inspired and encouraged by his interactions with Larry Adamson. Subsequently, after Mr. Adamson accepted the position as President of The Midnight Mission and, after their relationship grew, Mr. Adamson told Barry that he accepted the position because he could see how he could help him and others like him.

Eventually Barry was to be made the Mission's first Public Relations officer. He was responsible for media relations and giving tours. He arranged for people to come to the facility to see the work being done there.

"The bottom line of the program is that you have to take a journey of self-exploration. You have to look inward at all your defects of character. You have to come to grips with all the bad in you in order to scrape it away and become clean. I haven't touched drugs since I left The Midnight Mission. I own my own home. I've bought my own cars. Most importantly, I became a productive member of society again."

After leaving The Mission he went into the furniture business with Gerald Petrillo, a friend he thinks of as a brother, having gone through The Mission's program with him. He is now focusing more on his music career, performing with his band Blue Jelly. Blue Jelly is finishing its second CD that is called Live in Hell's Kitchen. While the title refers to New York City's infamous neighborhood, the songs are about Liss's experiences in Los Angeles's downtown area. Liss is also venturing into video production with CDs on fitness.

He calls himself The Second Chance Man and to return the favor for the second chance that The Mission gave him, he performs at The Mission during the holidays. His hope is that people will hear his story and be encouraged to keep up the hard work. "If it helps one person to see that that guy went through The Mission and to think to himself, 'Well, if this guy could do it, then maybe I can do it, too.' then it was worth my effort."

According to Barry, The Mission has taken in star basketball players, well-known musicians, doctors, lawyers and people from all walks of life. He muses, "I've been fortunate. Only one in ten make it. I'm sitting in my office in my house. I'm looking at my Queen Anne chairs and my beautiful, overpriced computers and my sound system. And I absolutely appreciate them too."

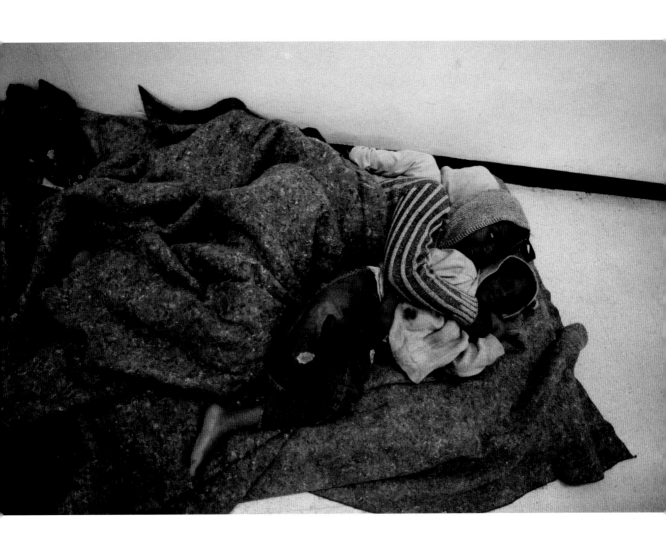

I began drinking and using at age 13 and I continued to drink and use for about 25 years with brief periods of abstinence, not recovery, at times wanting to stop but not knowing how. I was unwilling to feel the feelings, that's why I continued to drink and use. Whether it was disappointments or rejection or fear, whatever the case was, I'd get drunk or loaded and that was all that I would feel.

That continued. At first, the drugs and alcohol seemed to work for me. Because I didn't get arrested, I didn't beat anybody up, I didn't end up in the hospital, there were really no negative consequences tied to it initially. However, that quit working a long, long time ago. What's important for me to remember is not what the drugs and alcohol did for me because it stopped working for me a long time ago. It's what it did to me.

The death of both of my brothers is the direct result of this addiction: one was killed in a drunk driving accident. My other brother, in a relapse, took his life while under the influence. Also, during this period in my life, I was married but I took the addiction into my marriage so that was doomed from the beginning.

I had good jobs. I worked in the oil fields, I worked in logging camps, I worked in Alaska in lumber mills. I always had good jobs but I couldn't keep these jobs because Friday would begin my weekend and I wouldn't shut it down until Monday, sometimes Tuesday. Eventually those weekends started on Thursday and eventually it was every day.

After a while I just lost hope. I couldn't stand it anymore. I was tired of being drunk and loaded. I was tired of the effort it took to stay medicated. And that's when I found my way to a 12-step program and the process of surrender.

The Midnight Mission is a wonderful facility. The scale of the services provided here is unbelievable. The Reading Room is open to the community. They can come in here and get a break from the elements of the streets, whether heat or cold, and people have a chance to socialize. For the few hours that they're here they aren't using. And there is treatment and recovery happening all around them. Hopefully, they have their ears open and when they decide that they, too, would like to explore the change they know where to go.

Many of the people who use the Reading Room have seen peers that they ran the street with, that they used with, and they've seen their lives change. So it's a program of attraction. If I used to use and drink with you and I see that you're clean and sober and your life seems to be improving and your state of mind is improving, well, how did you do that?

When I went to a program I went because I just wanted to live. Period. And as a result of that choice and through the process of treatment and recovery my life has been blessed.

Today I have remarried. I have a beautiful wife, ShirleyAnn. I have custody of my son, Shane, and after 13 years of not seeing my daughter, Nicole, we have just begun to rebuild that relationship. Before I was a parent but now I am a father. That is the gift of recovery.

Don Halfenberg is a Certified Dependency Specialist and Program Manager at The Midnight Mission.

I've been trying to get sober for my entire adult life. I've been in nine different programs. I've been in recovery from age 30 to age 46 when I ended up at The Midnight Mission, never getting my sobriety because I never truly believed I was an alcoholic. I always thought, "Next time it's going to be different." But you know it always ends the same way — in jails or institutions.

I've always wanted to do it my way but eventually I found the willingness to try another way. I was willing to change. You can't change until you're ready, until you hit that final bottom when you've had enough. And, you know, I thought I hit that bottom nine different times but I guess I was just lying to myself. Finally, when I got to The Mission I was 46 years old, I was living on people's couches, pretty much not doing anything.

When I got to The Midnight Mission I learned the work ethic. I started working two weeks after I got here. I got a paying job. I learned how to save money. I learned how to open up a checking account. Now I even have a retirement fund so I've come a long way.

One thing that I've learned in sobriety is that I have to give it back or I'll lose what has been given to me. The way I give it back is: I went to school and now I give all my experience, knowledge and skills back to my clients. One of my clients has never had a job in his entire life, has been pushing a basket for the last 27 years. He has been here now, coming up on a year, he's going back to school, he's learning to be a truck driver and he has a girlfriend.

Jeff Mandel is a Certified Addiction Specialist and counselor at The Midnight Mission.

facing page : people served by The Midnight Mission.

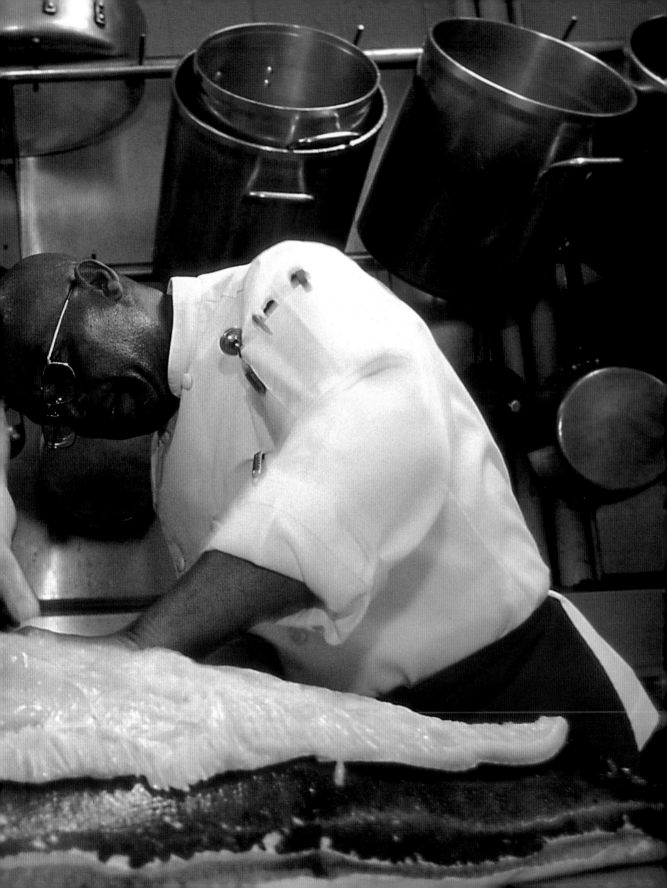

I come from the Midwest. I hear a lot of stories down here about bad childhoods, nightmare stories. Me, on the other hand, I came from a good Italian family. A lot of love. My grandparents raised me and gave me about everything I wanted. So my wrong turn in life has nothing to do with my upbringing.

When I was about 17 years old I went on the road playing pool. I was on the road for about 20 years and traveled all over the country. I made a lot of money. I've been on ESPN, the whole works.

I've been in a lot of world championships all around the country. Now, that lifestyle kept me in the fast lane. I was in the clubs drinking booze, a lot of things up the nose, the party life, it was all a part of that. It was a lot of fun for a lot of years. Then all of a sudden I crossed the invisible line with the drugs and the alcohol and it got to be an obsession with me. It got to the point where I forgot about my career. I forgot about my talents. I stopped playing professionally. I'd go to downtown areas and instead of playing I would hustle. I'd hustle just enough for my booze, my high and kick back and get snockered.

Anyhow that party lasted for 20 years. Ended up in L.A. over a girl I met on an Amtrak train who shook her ass and smiled at me just the right way.

So for 20 years I have been downtown, usually with money. If I wasn't working in a bar, there was usually a pool table. To make a long story short a little over a year ago I lost all interest in everything but the pipe and the booze. So I knew a few people who worked here at The Midnight, a few people I used to party with on the street that ended up coming to The Midnight and turned their lives around. I saw that it worked. I started coming in for meals, for refuge and one day I said you know what I'm gonna give this a whirl. Well The Midnight actually ended up saving my life.

Facing Page : Easter celebration at The Midnight Mission - volunteers serve food, Mr. T speaks with the staff, President Larry Adamson gives out candy ...

I graduated class of 1971 from high school. Drugs were plentiful and cheap and it was the thing to do. I had a blast! I went to college to stay out of Vietnam.

I married the minister's daughter in Redding, California and settled down. Somewhere along the line I crossed the line where drinking and drugs were something I did for fun to where it became something I had to do and I couldn't tell you when it was or how it happened.

Rick Baugh in his room at The Midnight Mission.

Practice hope. As hopefulness becomes a habit, you can achieve a permanently happy spirit.

// Norman Vincent Peale //

INDEX

❧

We could never learn to be brave and patient if there were only joy in the world.

// Helen Keller //

INDEX

᪥

Take the first step in faith.
You don't have to see the whole staircase, just take the first step.

// Dr. Martin Luther King, Jr. //

ACKNOWLEDGMENTS

❧

The author wishes to thank:

Larry Adamson, for having the vision to initiate this project, for the resources he made available and for the access he provided me to The Midnight Mission. Clancy Imislund, who provided valuable feedback to me during the project.

Larry Lyerla, for sharing his knowledge and insights with me and for his considerable time and energy in orienting me to Skid Row. The staff of The Midnight Mission, particularly Marcus Butler, William Day, William Dugar, Don Halfenberg, Gregg Johnson, Betsy Kelly, Jeff Mandel, Jessyka Quinteramora, Tyrone Robinson, Orlando Ward, Justin Wisniewski and Scott Yabroff.

I would also like to acknowledge Robert Balopole, Eric Bennett, Jeff Berke, Alicia Elkort, Jim Howat, Mary Kalifon, Jerry Lazar, Gary Marshall, Marty Ollstein, Helen Sanematsu, Greg Victoroff and Henry Wilson for their assistance.

Martin Elkort, of the prestigious New York Photo League, for his suggestions, prodding and assistance in editing the work.

My wife, Marge Brownstein, for her assistance with editing and her loving support.

David Garcia, Ernie Hill, Victoria Mulhall and Jeanette Rowe of the Los Angeles Homeless Services Agency. Their names were left out of the text for readability, but their assistance was invaluable.

Randy Walburger for his assistance at Palisades Park, Santa Monica.

The many wonderful people depicted in these photographs for their cooperation and permission. In some cases, I took photos without permission, as I often work in this way. I hope that no one is embarrassed by their appearance in this book. My only intention was to show what I saw and never to judge or ridicule.

Jim Reisman, owner of Trader Jim's Camera in Culver City, CA, who provided generous support of the project and his staff.